Brain Power

How to Improve Your Memory and Speed Reading Techniques Faster and More Efficiently

Sandra David

Copyright

ISBN 978-1-304-71476-3

Terms of Use

Any information provided in this book is through the author's interpretation. The author has done strenuous work to reassure the accuracy of this subject. If you wish you attempt any of the practices provided in this book, you are doing so with your own responsibility. The author will not be held accountable for any misinterpretations or misrepresentations of the information provided here.

All information provided is done so with every effort to represent the subject, but does not guarantee that your life will change. The author shall not be held liable for any direct or indirect damages that result from reading this book.

Contents

Introduction

Ever walked into a room and then could not remember why?

Ever gone to the store with a short list and realize when you get home that you have forgotten one or two things?

Do you struggle to remember names of the people that you just met?

That is awkward, especially in a work setting, is it not?

Is the only way you can remember phone numbers is to write them down?

Memory is a tricky thing. We might not remember what we ate for breakfast, but we can recall down to the last detail something that may have happened a week ago.

Some people seem to have a flawless memory, pulling up facts with ease about events from the past.

Granted, some people are wired to remember things easier, and so they can easier recall their memories while others have to think about it for a lot longer.

From remembering the groceries, to remembering meetings at work, our minds are always full of things that we must remember.

Some people have to write everything down, something that the digital age has helped with greatly, but still, it is time consuming to have to write everything down.

Thankfully, our brain is a mini supercomputer, and we can learn to improve our memory. We will help you learn some easy ways to learn how to improve your memory, so that you rely less and less on scribbled notes.

Better memory will help you in both your work and your home life.

Our brains are amazing, thanks to neuroplasticity, our brain is able to adapt to changes including, forming new neural pathways, alter existing connections and react and adapt to many situations, especially stimuli.

That is what we are going to be going over, to use the brain's natural ability to improve your memory skills.

Another aspect that we will go into for improvement is your reading speed.

We all know somebody who is done reading before the rest of us are even half-way through.

How can they do that? Are they pretending or do they really read that fast and do they retain what they have read?

The answer is that yes, they do read that fast and yes, they retain what they have read.

We will go over techniques to help improve your reading speed and retention as well.

Do not just wish you had the ability, unlock it.

From the Inside Out – Diet and Exercise

Before we go into the tips, tricks and exercises to improve your memory, you first need to make sure that your body is properly prepped for learning.

There is a very strong mind/body connection in humans and so what effects one, will affect the other.

Therefore, you want to improve one, you must also improve the other.

Do not worry, we are not talking about anything extensive or intensive, just some overall changes that will make it easier for you to learn new things, improve your memory and your overall health.

We will start with sleep. It is essential, we all need it, but we rarely seem to get enough, especially if you have a busy home life and work life that you are trying to juggle.

When we sleep, our brains are not overloaded with information from all five senses; our brains use that time to sort through, review, and store the information in the appropriate areas of our brain.

Furthermore, during our deepest stages of sleep is when the most memory-enhancing activity occurs.

When we are running low on sleep, we are not operating at our best; our abilities are diminished; especially in the areas of critical thinking, problem solving, creativity and our attention span.

When we get enough sleep, our brains will have small changes, those pathways necessary to remember things.

The more sleep we get, the stronger those pathways are, the better our memory.

Feeling groggy in the middle of the day?

If possible, opt for a short nap, around 10 minutes or so, instead of that afternoon caffeine.

Physical exercise is another part of keeping mentally fit. When you exercise, it increases the blood flow to all areas of the body, including the brain.

With increased blood flow, is increased oxygen flow, and that will improve your health, and your ability to learn.

Try to get between 15-30 minutes of exercise a day. You can take walks at lunchtime, take the stairs instead of the elevator, or even just do some basic stretches and movements. The idea is to get moving, increase the blood flow, and increase your health and your ability to learn.

You have heard the term brain food, but what does that really mean?

It means that there are certain foods that have health benefits, and brain foods are those foods that will help boost your health, especially your brain.

Let us start with the basics, a well-balanced diet, with moderate protein and a variety of vegetables, grains and fruits is not only essential for your overall health, but for healthy brain activity.

Alcohol, tobacco and caffeine all interfere with memory, so either cut them out or limit them.

Opt for water instead of soda; you should be drinking between 6-8 glasses of water a day.

You should limit your saturated fat and calorie intake as well.

Omega-3 fatty acids are beneficial to brain health. Not only will they boost your brainpower, but also they can lower your risk of developing Alzheimer's disease.

Fish is the best source of Omega-3 fatty acids, but if you do not like fish, it can also be found in walnuts, flaxseed oil, pumpkin seeds, and soybeans.

Leafy green vegetables are excellent choices; they are full of antioxidants, which will protect your brain cells from damage.

Add the following to your diet: bok choy, spinach, kale, sprouts, cabbage, collard greens, cauliflower, broccoli, arugula, romaine lettuce, and swiss chard.

Fruits with antioxidants include watermelon, cantaloupe, apricots, mangoes, plums, oranges, red apples, cherries, and grapes. Berries are a good source as well.

For supplements that boost brainpower, you can use the following: vitamin B12, vitamin B6, vitamin E, vitamin C, niacin, beta-carotene, iron, zinc, and ginkgo biloba.

Green tea is a source of polyphenols, which are antioxidants that will protect against free radicals. Free radicals can damage our brain cells. Green tea will help clear them from your system.

Check Your Stress at the Door

Stress, it is impossible to live without any stress, but it is possible to limit the stress that we have.

Stress will, over time, damage the hippocampus, the part of our brain that is involved with new memory formation and the retrieval of old ones.

Stress will also damage brain cells over the long term. Chronic stress will not only affect you mentally, but physically as well.

Chronic stress can lead to depression, symptoms of which include, difficulty concentrating, troubling remembering things, and difficulty focusing or concentrating on things.

If you are suffering from depression instead of just stress, please, see a doctor.

Treating depression results in a huge improvement in your cognitive abilities, including your memory.

One way to beat stress is to be social, being social will help keep both stress and depression at bay.

When you are feeling overwhelmed, find something fun to do with a friend or family member.

Take time to enjoy your life. If you let stress build up, it will make sleeping hard, starting a cycle of stress, insomnia, and lack of memory and cognitive functions.

Having an active social life, not only helps with your emotional health, but it helps with your mental health.

People with active social lives have a slower rate of memory decline than those who do not.

Anything that we enjoy, that gives us pleasure, stimulates our brains. Therefore, when we spend time with people who we enjoy, it stimulates our brains, helping keep it active and warding off against memory loss.

Do not forget the four-legged variety of friends, having a pet will not only increase your happiness factor and give you something to interact with, but it is a great stress reliever as well.

Part of enjoying your life is to foster a healthy and positive attitude. If you catch yourself with negative thoughts, strike them out.

Do not say things like "I have a bad memory" or "I cannot remember that".

Be confident that you will remember, even if it takes you a little while to recall the memory.

You must be confident that your brain is doing its job with storing things in your memory banks.

When you have a positive outlook and attitude, it makes it a lot harder to be worried about things that will cause you stress.

Laughter really is the best medicine; laughter will trigger multiple regions of the brain in a positive way, providing stimuli.

Try telling and listening to jokes, jokes, with their silly and pun-filled punch lines stimulate the creative parts in our brains as we try to work them out.

Do not let stress drag you down and make you blue, have a laugh and cheer up. Stop taking life so seriously, we only have one shot at it, make it enjoyable.

A happy mind is a mind that is healthy and open to remembering and learning.

Keep a reminder to be happy in your car, or your desk at work, such as a little toy or gadget, something that will bring a smile to your face when you need it the most.

Learn to laugh at yourself. Surround yourself with people with a sense of humor instead of those who do not have one.

Meditation is a much overlooked stress relief tool. People consider it too “new age” when in fact, meditation has been around for a very long time, and its benefits are time tested and proven.

Meditation can have health benefits such as improving our anxiety, chronic pain, depression, and high blood pressure. Meditation is a very effective way of halting a panic attack or anxiety attack.

Meditation, when done with breathing exercises will increase your blood flow, and the oxygen flow to your body and brain. Meditation helps to improve our concentration, creativity, focus, reasoning skills and our learning ability.

Meditation does more than just make us feel better; it produces changes in the brain over long-term practice. By meditating regularly, the area of the brain that is associated with feelings of peace and happiness, the prefrontal cortex, has more activity than those who do not.

Those who meditate often will also have a thicker cerebral cortex and more connections between their brain cells, which will help with their mental flexibility, alertness, and memory.

A meditation technique to help with stress and anxiety:

Find a comfortable spot. If you are at work, sit at your desk, feet flat on the floor, hands in your lap or resting on the armrests of the chair. If you are at home, you can either sit in a chair, cross-legged on the floor, or lay down. Make sure your clothing is not too tight or uncomfortable, as this will distract you.

Close your eyes. If you have trouble concentrating in the daylight, close the blinds or drapes if you are able. Start to relax, but if you are sitting, be careful to not slouch, lean back into the chair to avoid slouching. Just spend a few minutes sitting there with your eyes closed, relax any muscles that you feel are tense.

Take a deep breath and slowly let it out. Keep your mind still, focus only on your breathing, and clear your mind of anything that is worrying it. Put so much focus on your breathing, that your mind has no room for worries.

Breathe in and out slowly several times, at a pace that feels natural and calming to you. Focus only on your breathing, on the inhale and then the exhale.

Repeat whenever you feel stressed and to keep yourself from being stressed, we suggest doing this for 10 minutes every morning and every night.

Mnemonic Devices

There are tricks that you can use to help remember information, these are called mnemonic devices, and they are very useful for helping you remember certain things.

The various types of mnemonic devices that you can use and some examples of each are listed below.

Visual Image

When you associate a visual image with a word or a name, it can help you remember easier. Visual images are easier for us to remember than words, so by using your imagination to make mental images, and then associating them with what you want to remember, you will be able to remember easier, by bringing up the image when you see the thing or person that you have associated with that image.

Some tips for making associations between images:

Have a vivid and clear imagine in your mind, with as much detail as possible. Include as many senses as possible such as sound, touch, texture, taste or smell

Make the image evoke an emotion; avoid negative emotions though. Make it a positive or humorous emotion.

Make sure that the two items that you are picturing are interacting in some way, which strengthens the bond between the two in your mind. For example, to remember Rosa Parks, think of a Rose, in a car, parking in a parking lot.

Use action, relate the two images with having something happen, an action of some sort, this will also make it easier to remember.

If you make the images unusual, such as things that are not possible, or are just silly and bizarre, that increases the chances of you remembering it. Exaggerate features or things that you want to remember, make it unusual and fun. For example, for elongate, you can think of a very long letter E, that serves as a gate.

You can substitute words or a word that sound similar or are similar in meaning to help you remember.

Rhymes and Songs

You can use rhymes, alliteration, jokes, and songs to help remember. This is a fun way to help remember things, especially for creative people, the possibilities are endless. As children, we learn the alphabet by singing it, not just repeating it.

We remember how many days are in each month by using the rhyme we learn in school, thirty days hath September, April, June, and November.

The multiplication table can be easily memorized by the use of simple rhymes; eight and eight fell on the floor, when they got up, they were sixty-four. Some more uses:

Distinguish between similar sounding words: Here or Hear = we hear with our ear

Using a word within a word to remember:

When you assume you make and ass of u and me

A secretary must keep a secret

Sequences of letters: Where ever there is a Q, there is a U too

Acrostics (Sentences)

Acrostics are when you make up a sentence using the first letter of each word that you are trying to remember.

This is a very simple thing to do and to memorize and is very useful when you need to remember a list or the order of things in a specific order.

Acrostics is less limiting than other methods, but more thought might have to be put into it to come up with them, and it will require you to remember a whole sentence, so make it unusual and fun, that makes it easier to remember.

Some examples:

To remember the directions on a compass: Never eat Shredded Wheat (North, East, South, West)

The oceans: I am a person (Indian, Arctic, Atlantic, Pacific)

Use acrostics for names that you want to remember, company names and organizations, places, and dates.

When picking out the words to use, use positive words, fun words, and words with action or emotion. Have fun with it.

Acronyms

An acronym is where you take the first letter of all the key words that you want to remember and create a new word with them.

This is a very good tool for remembering words in a very specific order.

You run across acronyms all the time and probably do not realize it, as they have become part of our everyday language, such as SCUBA (Self

Contained Underwater Breathing Apparatus) and LASER (Light Amplification by Stimulated Emission of Radiation).

We see it all the time with sports Associations such as NBA (National Basketball Association) and NHL (National Hockey League).

You can use Acronyms to help remember things, such as the great lakes; use the word HOMES to remember that the Great Lakes are Huron, Ontario, Michigan, Erie, and Superior.

There are some disadvantages to Acronyms, like acrostics, they help use memorize, but not understand.

They have no role in our comprehension of things, only our memory of the words.

Another problem with Acronyms is that they can be difficult to form; no all lists of words will be able to spell out a new word that you can memorize to help you to remember the list. In this way, Acronyms can be limited.

Chunking

Chunking is a technique mostly used for numbers, although it can be used for other things, such as grocery lists, where you break the items into categories such as fruits, vegetables, meat, etc.

Chunking is where you take individual pieces of information and group them together so that they are easier to remember.

By breaking a long list of numbers or other information into smaller sections, or chunks, it makes it easier to remember.

Take telephone numbers for example, instead of remembering it as one string of numbers, think of it as group of three, another group of three and then a group of four, remembering three groups of information is easier for our brains that just one large number.

Method of Loci

This method combines visual memory and association. This requires you to recall a path that you walk often, and are well familiar with, such as a walk up the path to your house, and around the house, or the park that you either walk or jog daily, or if you walk to work or school, the route that you take.

For this to work you must know this path, the landmarks, the things that do not change on this path.

You will need one landmark (mailbox, planter, table, picture, etc.) that is always on that path for each item that you need to remember.

Now, visualize each item or idea that you want to remember, along that path. So meeting, imagine, vividly, each point that you want to make at a different spot along this path so as you need to remember, start at the beginning and make your mental journey along the path, seeing each item along the way.

Names, Places and Numbers

Names

Remembering names is a very useful tool, very few times are we lucky enough to be where everybody is wearing a nametag and we must draw from our memory who each person is.

To begin with, always make sure that you are paying attention to them when they say their name, seems so basic that we almost should not have to mention it, but many people just do not pay attention when they learn somebody's name.

If you do not catch their name, ask again.

Use the FACE method (focus, ask, comment and employ). Focus, makes sure you are watching their face when they say their name.

Ask, clarify the name if you are not sure if you have heard it correctly, or to inquire if they have a preferred nickname.

Comment, say something that includes their name, and associate with something else in your head, "I used to play tennis with somebody named Ted".

Employ, make sure you use the name to reinforce the memory, "it was very nice to meet you Ted".

Without overdoing it, repeat their name during your conversation, just a few times, to help you associate their name with their face.

As you converse with them, pick out a fact or two about that person and associate it with their name.

For instance, if they mention a hobby, or their career, you can link the two together to double your chances of remembering their names.

Use alliteration or mnemonic devices to help you remember. Simple word association tricks can be very useless. Gus drives a bus; Jackie from Jersey, Taylor is a tailor, salesman Stan, etc.

In a business setting, always get a business card, and so you have something tangible to associate with their face and name.

Use mental associations and imagery to help remember names. John Green for example, picture him wearing all green, even with green hair.

Associate their name with a body part, for example, Adam's Adams Apple, or Harry's hair. Associate them with well-known people, so for example, somebody named Teresa, associate them with the image of mother Teresa.

For last names, you can break the name into words and associate it that way, for Beachcomber, imagine a large comb, combing the beach.

Places

How often do you waste time, searching for something that you cannot find, such as your keys, or a memo at work.

It is very frustrating to have to try to fumble and search for it, especially if you need it now.

The best way to avoid this is to organize. A messy house or a messy desk is an open invitation to disaster when it comes to finding things quickly.

Make a place for everything, and keep it there. Resist the urge to clutter.

Spending some time making sure that your home, office, and car are organized is the best way to prevent the frantic search for things.

Get a file box instead of shoving paperwork into a drawer. Hang your coat up; stop throwing them in a pile on the couch.

For common items, like your keys, purse, glasses, phone, etc., use a memory spot. A memory spot is a designated place to always put that specific item.

A bowl on the counter for your car keys, a hook in the closet for you purse are two examples.

If you have a permanent spot for each item and you always use that spot, you will never have to search through your house, car, or office again.

Hang up a key holder by the front door for keys; have a hook installed in a closet for your purse, use only one table to set your reading glasses on, etc.

Another way to help remember is association. Associate the item that you are setting down, with the object that you are setting in on.

For example, if you set your purse down on the coffee table, imagine your purse swimming in a giant cup of coffee. If you throw your wallet into the sock drawer, imagine your wallet wearing a sock.

Numbers

One way of memorizing numbers to visualize the shape the numbers would make on a keypad. This works great for short numbers, like a zip code, PIN number, or access code.

Using associate helps remember numbers as well. Find a connection between the number that you want to memorize and a number that you already have associated with something else, like dates, or the number of your favorite sport's figure.

We have already gone over chunking, but for numbers, it is really one of the best ways to be able to remember the information. Learn to use it.

Look for patterns in the numbers. Is there a pattern, such as a sequence of all odd numbers, or in sequence? You can use word association with this to build up a small, easy to remember story in your head about the numbers to help you remember.

Do not just read them, write it down, or say it out loud. That helps to reinforce the memory and the number by actively paying attention to it.

This goes hand in hand with repetition, the more you repeat something, and the more apt you are to remember it. So write it down a few times, or say it out loud several times.

More Simple Memory Tricks

We have gone over how to improve your memory by taking care of your body and de-stressing yourself.

We have gone over mnemonic devices and simple ways to help remember names, locations, and numbers.

Now, we will go over all of the rest of the miscellaneous tips and tricks to improving your memory.

Memory is a "use it or lose it" mental muscle. If you do not use your brainpower, it gets weaker, so the more you use your brain, the stronger it will become; therefore, the more your memory will improve.

By keeping your brain stimulated, you will help keep your neural pathways engaged and encourage new neural pathway growth.

What type of mental stimulation should you engage in to flex your mental muscle?

Look for something that falls into each of these three categories:

1. It has to be something totally new to you. If it is something that you are familiar with already, it

will not engage your brain muscles. It has to be something you are totally unfamiliar with, like learning a new language, a new sport, or a new hobby.

2. It has to be something that is challenging. It has to be something that makes your brain work. Puzzles such as crosswords, logic puzzles and Sudoku all are challenging; they engage your brain. Trivia games as well will work for this.

3. You have to enjoy it. It has to be something that you will enjoy doing. An interested brain is an engaged brain.

Your memory is very much cued into your senses. The more sensory input that you have, the more apt you are to remember it. Pay attention to how things taste, smell, feels as well as how it looks and it will be easier to recall those memories.

Paying attention is vital to being able to memorize. Improve your focus, and improve your memory.

When in a meeting, or on the phone, or anytime you are supposed to be listening to one thing, pull your focus onto the speaker.

Tune out the background noise, stop letting yourself be sidetracked, and pay attention to what you are listening too.

The same goes for visual memory; you can actually improve your visual memory by practicing a few of these exercises:

Open up a magazine, find a full-page picture, and study it for about five minutes. Then flip the magazine over and on a piece of paper, list as many things as you can remember about the picture. Set a timer for two minutes and write as many details as you remember. Do this once a day, using a different picture each time.

Practice your observation skills by walking into a room and take note of the details. What colors are used, where the furniture is placed, etc.? Do this whenever you go someplace new, take about 45 seconds to just take it in, the details of it.

We all learn in different ways. Some of us learn by doing, some by reading, and some by hearing.

If you learn by doing, kinesthetic learning, then you learn better when you interact with something, rather than hear or read about it.

If you are more of an auditory learner, find the information in audio form or video form and listen to it.

Visual learners prefer to read to learn. Always try to process the information that you need to remember in the way that you learn the fastest and the easiest.

Learn to be an active listener.

Do not just lend half an ear when somebody talks, pay attention.

Active listening is more than just following along the conversation and nodding your head, it means you interact with the speaker.

Do not interrupt them, but give them your full attention, ask them to elaborate on things that you do not fully understand.

This is the digital age; use it to help you remember things.

There are numerous apps that can be downloaded onto your phone and computer that will synch up and help you remember dates, appointments, to-do lists and pretty much anything else that you might need to do.

Brain Boosting Exercises

From fun to difficult, here are some things that you can do to help improve your memory and flex your mental muscles.

These are things that range from simple and fast to complicated and will be a long-term project, find the ones that suit you the best.

Use your other hand. If you are right-handed, try brushing your teeth, brushing your hair or eating with your left hand. Try using your non-dominant hand more; it will force your brain to work as you try to co-ordinate the hand you are not used to doing things with. This can be frustrating, and in the case of eating, messy, but it really is a simple and great way to make your brain work

Speaking of messy, try eating with your eyes closed. You will sharpen your other senses while doing this, and since you are relying on your other senses, it makes your brain work because you are doing something you are used to doing, a different way.

Learn a new word every day. You can get a daily calendar, pick a random word from the dictionary, or sign up on online to receive a new word a day through your email. Not only will this help boost your brainpower, but it makes you smarter as well.

Pick up a book that is about something you would normally not read, or watch documentaries. You will learn something new, and might even enjoy yourself at the same time.

Make it a musical quiz! Dig out your cd's or queue up some of your songs from your youth on your computer or mp3 player. Start a song, and then stop it at random places and try to remember the next line. If you love movies, play a movie and then stop it and see if you remember the next line that comes.

The make games called Scene It that are based on movie trivia; these are both fun and help improve memory and brainpower.

Make some flash cards. Yes, you heard that right, only instead of trying to remember the multiplication table or vocabulary words, pick a topic that you do not know much about, but want to learn about. Maybe a country you have wanted to visit, or a band you like, etc. Spend some time doing some research and make a set of flash cards about facts related to that topic. Keep the flash card questions and answers simple and short. Every now and then, get your flash cards out and see how much you remember.

Simon says! Remember that game, the electronic version, with the blinking lights and you had to copy the exact sequence and it would get more and more complicated? Find a copy of the game and play it. It is an excellent way to help improve your short-term memory, and it can be fun as well.

Practice shopping with no lists. Make a grocery list and then either put it in your purse, or in your wallet and then go to the store. See if you can remember everything on the list, and only until you are ready to checkout do you pull out your list and see how close you got. Do this every time you go shopping, it will help boost your brainpower, and once again, help your short-term memory.

Buy a book of logic problems, Sudoku, or crossword puzzles and work one puzzle a day.

Read a mystery book and try to figure out who did it.

Find an online site with brain games. There are many websites out there full of fun and engaging memory games for both kids and adults and most are free to play. After work, spend about 15 minutes playing memory games online, it will be fun, and it will help you reduce your stress.

Find something to write about. When we write, we engage the thinking part of our brain, especially if we try to use good grammar and new vocabulary words. Keep a daily journal, or get back in touch with friends and family with email or through written letters. Write stories or even start a blog and write about what you feel like writing about.

Introduction to Speed Reading

When we read, we read a word or two, our eyes stop, and that stop is when we process the information that we have just read, so we read another word or two, and so on.

Speed reading is when any number of techniques is used that will increase our rate of reading, without losing our ability to comprehend.

We tend to focus on every word and space when we read, speed reading occurs when the number of stops that our eye makes is minimized.

What are the advantages of speed reading?

When you are able to double your reading rate, it means you process more information in less time.

You would have less time spent on reading and more time to do the things that you want to do.

Speed reading is extremely useful when you are working, especially if your job involves large quantities of paperwork that must be read and then handled.

You can also use some speed reading techniques, such as skimming, to quickly go through paperwork and grasp the basic idea of it.

First, we recommend that you discover what your reading speed is.

The average reading speed is 250 words per minute, or about half a page of a book per minute.

Get a book and count the number of words that are on the page.

Write it down. Get a timer and set it for one minute, start the timer and begin to read.

When the timer stops, see how many words you managed to read in that minute, that is your reading speed.

Many people, when they read, say each word in their head as they read it.

This actually slows down your reading speeding, speed readers have learned to recognize the word as whole, not reading each word out loud.

By identifying words without focusing on each letter, not sounding out all the words, skimming small sections, not sounding out all the words, not sub-vocalizing all the phrases you can increase your reading speed.

You will need a distraction free spot in order to learn to increase your reading speed.

No background sounds such as TV, music or even talking from others if you can help it.

Find a quiet spot that will be comfortable, have your cell phone off, as few distractions as possible.

If you need to, use earplugs to block out the background noise.

Not all material is appropriate for speed reading. Material with a large amount of very detailed data in it, are not good materials to practice or even speed reading techniques on.

Legal paperwork, detailed reports, financial data reports are all examples of when you should not utilize speed reading techniques.

You need to be able to focus, to remember, and to analyze as you read for things such as those.

Practice makes perfect, so you will have to practice often in order to re-train your brain to increase your reading speed.

Practice twenty to thirty minutes per day or every other day.

Do not practice with a textbook or a complicated book to begin with.

Pick a novel, or non-fiction that does not require extra concentration.

Re-test your reading speed once a week to track your progress, have you increased your speed any?

Speed Reading Basics

To begin with, practice focusing not on one word at a time, but on chunks of words, or several words at once.

See a group of words and try to comprehend the meaning of the words without having to read each word in your head.

Increase the number of words that you recognize slowly, start with two at a time, then as it gets easier, work up to three, then four, etc.

Learn to scan the words without spending extra thought on the way they are pronounced, or the meaning of each word.

As long as you recognize the word, you know what it means; you do not have to give extra thought to it.

With time and practice, you will be able to read entire sentences and even short paragraphs instantly.

Using your hand to guide you as you practice and learn this skill will help you.

No matter what you are reading, there will be a lot of non-useful information buried in the information that matters.

Once you get better at reading words and phrases without reading each word, then you can quickly learn to tell if a sentence, or even a paragraph will be useful to read, or if it is just filler material.

When you get to something important, then you can slow down.

Skimming is the technique where you search for relevant words or phrases in the text.

It is also used help identify material that is not as useful, so that you can skip it, and continue onto the part of the text that you need to focus on.

Skimming is useful when you want to decide the gist of the material and if you want to spend more time reading it more in depth or not.

To skim follow these steps:

Read the title, introduction, and the subheadings of the material or book. Take a minute to thing about how they are related to the topic.

Read the first sentence in each paragraph only, do this for the entire book, article or material that you have to read. If that is not enough information, you can choose to read both the first sentence and the last sentence of each and every paragraph.

Skim the book or material again, looking for words that usually signify importance, such as proper nouns, numbers, words that will tell you who, what, where, how and why, adjectives, and font changes such as italics or bold. Use your word recognize skills as you skim to decide what words to hone in on.

Read the last paragraph or the summary in its entirety.

If you are looking for a specific thing in the material, such as a specific fact or piece of information, then you can use scanning to find it. Scanning will take practice, but it allows you to go through a large section of text quickly.

How to use scanning:

Know what it is you are looking for first of all and keep it in your mind what it is that you are scanning the material to find. This is to prevent you from being distracted by irrelevant information.

Identify any keywords that will help you key in on this information. Know what words you are looking for, will it be a number, a place, a date or a person's name, etc.

Read the material, scanning over several lines of text at one time.

When you spot a keyword, read the sentence that contained that word, and sometimes the one before and after it to truly make sure that you have the right information.

Use your hand, or a pen to guide your eyes along the page so that you are using your eyes in a smooth motion. You can either run your hand under the words as you read, or down the side of the book. Our eyes will track movement automatically, so if you use a pen or our hand, it naturally will draw our attention to the movement, and we follow along with it. This technique is called meta guiding.

Here are some techniques that involve using meta guiding:

Move your hand diagonally down the page, reading only the words that your hand crosses.

This is a good way to get a basic feel for the information on the page, and does not work for fact-laden materials, but it will give you a feel for the type of information on the page.

Use your fingertip to skip words in groups of 4-6 words at a time.

You eye will follow your fingers. Do not hop in too big of a chunk, or you could miss vital information, but it is a great way to skip words and phrases that are more filler than useful and to quickly read a page.

Breaking Bad Reading Habits

Learning to speed read is not as much about learning new ways to read, as it is about breaking the reading habits that you already have.

When you break the bad reading habits, you are able to read faster and with more efficiency.

When you pronounce each word in your head as you read it, that is called sub-vocalization, and it is the number one reason for why your reading speed is likely slow.

As you read, you hear the voice in your head, for each word.

This slows you down because you can understand words faster than you can say them.

You see the word "rabbit" and you know instantly what a rabbit is and it is instant recognition of the word itself and its meaning.

It takes you longer to say the word "rabbit" than it does for you to see the word and comprehend what the word is and what it refers to.

When you sub-vocalize, you limit your reading speed to only as fast as you can speak the words.

The good news is, once you realize that you are sub-vocalizing, and then it becomes easier to turn off that voice in your head that is slowing you down. When you realize that you are doing it, focus on NOT doing it.

When you start reading by blocks on words, it will further help you learn to not vocalize, since you cannot say more than one word at once, out loud or in your head.

This will probably be one of the toughest bad habits to overcome because when we are little and learning to read, we learn to read the words out loud.

As we get older, we might move our lips, but then we tend to sub-vocalize instead of reading out loud or moving our lips, but the outcome is the same, we are stuck reading only at the pace that we can speak at.

Practice reading and not saying the words in your head, learn how to stop doing that and you will increase your reading speed greatly.

Do not give up, practice is the way to go for this bad habit, the more you practice and focus on not sub-vocalizing, the more you will not do it.

Learn to read blocks of words, or chunking your words together instead of reading word by word.

You actually have a better reading comprehension when you read in blocks of words or a full sentence at once because you are not focusing on each and every word and what each word means.

When you break the habit of reading each word individually, you increase both your speed and comprehension of reading.

Practice reading two words at a time first, then when comfortable doing it that way, increase by one word.

It may help you to hold the book back further from you than normal, not so far that you strain your eyes, but just enough so that you are able to focus on a larger area of text than just a few words at a time.

If you are having trouble focusing, get your eyes checked. Bad eyesight is the biggest cause of why speed reading is hard for some people to learn.

Learn to make each eye movement count. When you focus on each word and each space, it takes a long time to read a sentence, let alone a book.

Our eyes can take in more information than just one word at time; we just do not do that, because we are not taught that we can!

We are taught to read, one word at a time and nothing more.

We can actually “see” four-six words at once, or about one and half inches at a time.

We can also use our peripheral vision to see the words just outside of that vision span.

To help your eye “see” more than one word at a time, relax your facial muscles and soft of let your gaze fall upon the chunk of text, instead of focusing on just one word.

Ever try to see the image in the 3-D Magic Eye pictures?

Where you sort of let your eyes un-focus and a shape takes form from the pattern?

This is the same concept here with seeing blocks of words instead of individual words.

We tend to not just read, but to re-read as we read.

When we got back and re-read material that we have already read, that is called regression and it is unnecessary.

Sometimes we will do it because we want to verify that we read something right, or to make sure that we understand it fully, especially if we are reading something new that we are trying to learn.

Often, we do this without even realizing that we are doing it, it is a bad habit that we do not even realize we have, or if we are stressed, tired, or just not focused, it becomes more common.

If you use a pointer, pen, or your finger to run along the words, it will stop you from going back to re-read, as your eyes will be following along with the movement on the page, going forwards, not back.

Conclusion

Memory is a tricky thing; it can be our biggest ally or our biggest foe.

Having a good memory, in short, just makes life easier.

We can rely on our gadgets and gizmos to help us keep track of our lives, but there is no digital substitute for having a good memory.

A good memory can make our days run more efficiently and smoothly.

How wonderful would it be to go to the grocery store and not have to stop in the middle of an aisle, while you tried to figure out which four things you needed, or fumbling for you list or phone to pull of your digital list of needed items.

Life is much easier when we can just run into the store without having to be frustrated or fumbling for a list.

A good memory can save us from the mental stuttering and fumbling of trying to remember who somebody is when they can clearly remember you and you are at a loss.

This is especially awkward when it happens in a work related situation!

From making things easier at home, to making us more efficient at our jobs, a good memory is a necessity.

We know why it is important, and now you know how to boost that brain power and improve your memory.

From feeding your mind and your body well, you can cultivate a good memory on a foundation of a healthy brain and body.

Your body is a complex machine, with the brain at the center of it; all parts must be healthy in order for it to work well.

Take care of the body, and the brain will stay healthy. Stress is a huge factor in degrading memory functions, as is lack of sleep.

We have helped you learn specific ways to help you remember information.

It is up to you to practice them and to put them to good use.

Speed reading does not involve your memory, but it does involve your brain power.

Learning to speed read is not so much about a specific technique as much as it is learning new reading habits.

Most of us still read the same way we learned to when we were children, word by word and saying the word in our heads as we read.

Now you know that there are other ways to read, and indeed, comprehend.

Make your time more efficient by finding what you are looking for on a page, or in an article faster.

www.ingramcontent.com/pod-product-compliance
Ingram Content Group UK Ltd.
Pitfield, Milton Keynes, MK11 3LW, UK
UKHW041838200726
13854UKWH00003BA/1193